Wellness Recovery Action Plan®

A system for monitoring, reducing and eliminating uncomfortable or dangerous physical and emotional difficulties

Mary Ellen Copeland PhD

**author of *The Depression Workbook:
A Guide to Living with Depression and Manic
Depression* and *Living Without Depression and
Manic Depression:
A Guide to Maintaining Mood Stability***

Peach Press

*This book is dedicated to
Jane Winterling who provided inspiration and
ideas for this book, Alan McNabb who named
the plan WRAP®, numerous reviewers, editors,
and all the dedicated people who attended the
eight day Recovery Series in Bradford, Vermont
for their persistence in finding a system
that really worked.*

CONTENTS

PREFACE

I've been working with people who experience mild to severe psychiatric symptoms, often exacerbated by a wide variety of physical ailments, as well as with people who experience chronic pain, for nine years.

This work is a result of my ongoing personal search for wellness and improvement in the quality of my life in spite of being diagnosed with manic depression, major depression, fibromyalgia and chronic myofascial pain syndrome.

Fifteen years ago, many years of high achievement and life enjoyment turned into confusion, frustration and pain. I was unhappy with this unanticipated turn of events. I wanted my life back, to work and to play, to enjoy my family and friends.

My attempts to find out how people with these kinds of disorders cope on a day-to-day basis only served to increase my frustration. My psychiatrist first promised me this information, then told me that none existed. My "medical" doctor tried valiantly to convince me that the severe pain and other mysterious symptoms that were physically disabling me were "all in my head."

My persistence in searching for answers and compiling my findings for my own use, and for use by others, has led me on a rich and rewarding journey that has confirmed and affirmed my belief in the richness of the human experience. From publishing houses to major medical centers, from the backwoods of Alaska to the back wards of psychiatric hospitals, I have been privileged to be invited into the lives of people whose courage and persistence continue to impress and inspire me.

Through this process of networking recovery information, I have uncovered ideas and strategies that, while often very simple and very safe, have the capacity to create major life change. I continue to search for these strategies, share them with others, and now I am teaching others to be mental health educators.

A group I was working with in Bradford, Vermont complained that the wellness process was all too confusing. Through their prodding and hard work, and the efforts of a very skilled mental health worker, we have come up with a system that people are finding works for them.

This system has been so enthusiastically received that I decided to publish and distribute it so that it would be widely available. While I specifically developed it to be used by people who experience psychiatric symptoms, people with all kinds of health conditions, and even some who have no significant complaints but want to stay healthy, have found this system to be valuable. An optional new section, Post Crisis Planning, is included here. The need for the addition of an optional new section, Post Recovery Planning, to the Wellness Recovery Action Plan, was brought to my attention by Richard Hart, a Mental Health Recovery Facilitator from West Virginia.

I use my WRAP plan consistently myself. It works very well for me. When things are starting to "go down the drain," my partner says, "Where's your WRAP?"

Overall Description

The Wellness Recovery Action Program is a structured system for monitoring uncomfortable and distressing symptoms and, through planned responses, reducing, modifying or eliminating those symptoms. It also includes plans for responses from others when your symptoms have made it impossible for you to continue to make decisions, take care of yourself and keep yourself safe. Anecdotal reporting from people who are using this system indicates that, by helping them feel prepared, it is working for them by helping them to feel better more often and by improving the overall quality of their life.

This system was developed by people who have been dealing with a variety of psychiatric symptoms for many years and are working hard to feel better and get on with their lives. I have shared it with people with other illnesses and they feel that it can be easily adapted for use with other disorders.

Using a three ring binder, a set of tabs or dividers, and lined three ring paper, a Wellness Toolbox and six part monitoring and response system is developed by the person who experiences the symptoms. This person may be assisted in this process by the supporters and health care professionals *of their choice*.

Section 1 is a daily maintenance plan. Part 1 is a description of how you feel when you feel well. Part 2 is a list of everything you need to do every day to maintain your wellness. Part 3 is a list of things you might need to consider doing that day.

Section 2 deals with triggers. Part 1 identifies those events or situations which, if they occur, might cause uncomfortable symptoms to begin. Part 2 is a plan of what to do if any of these triggers occur.

Section 3 deals with early warning signs. Part 1 involves identification of those subtle signs that may indicate the situation is beginning to worsen. Part 2 is a plan of what to do if any of these early warning signs are noticed.

Section 4 deals with symptoms that occur when the situation has gotten much worse but has not yet reached a crisis, where you can still take action in your own behalf. Part 2 is a plan of what to do if any of these symptoms occur.

Section 5 is the crisis plan. It identifies those symptoms that indicate you can no longer continue to make decisions, take care of yourself and keep yourself safe. It is for use by supporters and health care professionals on your behalf as the person who developed the plan.

The planning process begins by developing a Wellness Toolbox, a listing of skills and strategies that you have used or want to use to keep yourself well and to help yourself feel better when you do not feel well.

Part 1 is information that defines what you are like when you are well. Part 2 identifies those symptoms that indicate others need to take over responsibility for your care. Part 3 names those supporters and identifies their roles. Part 4 identifies those medications which, if necessary, are alright with you, those which are not, and the reasons why. Part 5 gives you the option of developing a home, community care or respite center plan to use, if possible, instead lieu of hospitalization. Part 6 identifies the treatment facilities which, if necessary, are alright with you, those which are not, and the reasons why. Part 7 identifies the treatments which, if necessary, are alright with you, those which are not, and the reasons why. Part 8 is an intensive description of what is wanted from supporters—and what is not wanted—when symptoms become this intense. Part 9 gives information for supporters to use in determining when you no longer need to use your crisis plan.

Section 6, Post Crisis Planning is a more recent addition to the plan. It is different from other sections of your Wellness Recovery Action Plan in that it is constantly changing as you heal. For instance, it is anticipated that two weeks after the crisis you will be feeling much better than you did after one week and therefore your daily activities would be different. The post crisis form leads you through the process of outlining your own post crisis plan.

Who Could Use WRAP®?

The answer to the question who could use this plan is simple. This plan could be used by anyone who wants to create positive change in the way they feel, or increase their enjoyment of life. It may mean they want to effectively manage certain aspects of their lives to decrease the intensity of physical or psychological pain-anything from depression to arthritis, from panic attacks to diabetes—or increase their level of wellness. It may mean they want to decrease the occurrence rate of acute episodes of an illness such as bipolar disorder, asthma or fibromyalgia. I have described this plan at workshops and conferences and the response is always the same. "This is something I can do for myself, something that will work."

The following example will help you be aware of how this plan can help when trying to avoid, or addressing a condition that seems to be rampant in our fast paced society. It is aptly called "burn-out" and it is caused by working too hard or under too much stress without taking time to take care of yourself. Burn-out, if not addressed will interfere with day to day functioning, and might even cause a serious illness.

The symptoms of burn out often mimic a physical or psychological disorder. They include:
> irritability
> disturbed sleep
> increased anxiety
> poor memory
> feeling "spaced out"
> feeling like a failure at everything
> feeling overwhelmed
> feeling emotionally disconnected to things that have meaning in life
> decreased ability to make decisions
> racing thoughts
> anger

edginess
nothing seems worthwhile
feeling helpless, hopeless and worthless

As you think about your symptoms, you may realize you are becoming burned out or are already burned out. Then you would develop your book to address burn out.

Unfortunately, many people respond to burn out by trying harder at everything, a strategy that is bound to fail. Your plans of what you need to do for yourself might include:

> stopping or decreasing the amount of time spent dealing with work and other responsibilities
> rest
> talking and crying time (see peer counseling in the Appendix)
> a variety of creative activities (see creative activities in the Appendix)
> avoidance of activities that increase stress
> giving yourself permission to say "no."

If you follow your plans, you will notice that the feelings that indicated you are burned out will begin to abate. If they don't, you may need to change your plans, work with a section toward the back of your book that includes more direction, or see a health care professional.

Getting Started

You can use any notebook or paper to develop your Wellness Recovery Action Plan. You can also develop it on your computer or tape record your responses. However, most people have found it most convenient to use a ring type binder—one inch thick will do—dividers or tabs, a supply of binder filler paper and a writing instrument of some kind. You may also choose to have a friend or other supporter give you assistance and feedback—but this is up to you. If you don't like to write, you could ask someone else to write your plan down for you as you tell them what to say .

CHAPTER 1

Developing a Wellness Toolbox

The first step in developing your own Wellness Recovery Action Plan, is to develop a Wellness Toolbox. This is a listing of things you have done in the past, or could do, to help yourself stay well; and, things you could do to help yourself feel better when you are not doing well. You will use these "tools" to develop your own WRAP.

Insert several sheets of paper in the front of your binder. List on these sheets the tools, strategies and skills you need to use on a daily basis to keep yourself well, along with those you use frequently or occasionally to help yourself feel better and to relieve troubling symptoms. Include things that you have done in the past, things that you have heard of and thought you might like to try, and things that have been recommended to you by health care providers and other supporters. You can get ideas on other tools from self-help books including those by Mary Ellen Copeland including: *The Depression Workbook: A Guide to Living With Depression and Manic Depression*, and *Living Without Depression and Manic Depression: A Guide to Maintaining Mood Stability*, *The Worry Control Book*, *Winning Against Relapse*, *Healing the Trauma of Abuse*, and *The Loneliness Workbook*. You can get other ideas from the audio tapes *Winning Against Relapse Program* and *Strategies for Living with Depression and Manic Depression*.

The following list includes the tools that are most commonly used to stay well and help relieve symptoms. If the tool is preceded by an asterisk, you can find more information in the appendix.

- Talk to a friend—many people find this to be really helpful
- Talk to a health care professional

- *Peer counseling or exchange listening
- *Focusing exercises
- *Relaxation and stress reduction exercises
- *Guided imagery
- *Journaling—writing in a notebook
- *Creative affirming activities
- *Exercise
- *Diet considerations
- *Light through your eyes
- *Extra rest
- Take time off from home or work responsibilities
- Hot packs or cold packs
- Take medications, vitamins, minerals, herbal supplements
- Attend a support group
- See your counselor
- Do something "normal" like washing your hair, shaving or going to work
- Get a medication check
- Get a second opinion
- Call a warm or hot line
- Surround yourself with people who are positive, affirming and loving
- Wear something that makes you feel good
- Look through old pictures, scrapbooks and photo albums
- Make a list of your accomplishments
- Spend ten minutes writing down everything good you can think of about yourself
- Do something that makes you laugh
- Do something special for someone else
- Get some little things done
- Repeat positive affirmations
- focus on and appreciate what is happening right now
- Take a warm bath
- Listen to music, make music or sing

Your list of tools could also include things you want to avoid like:

- alcohol, sugar and caffeine

- going to bars
- getting overtired
- certain people

Refer to these lists as you develop your Wellness Recovery Action Plan. Keep it in the front of your binder so you can use it whenever you feel you need to revise all or parts of your plan.

CHAPTER 2

Daily Maintenance Plan

You may have discovered that there are certain things you need to do every day to maintain your wellness. Writing them down and reminding yourself daily to do these things is an important step toward wellness. A daily maintenance plan helps you recognize those things which you need to do to remain healthy, and then to plan your days accordingly. Also, when things have been going well for a while and you notice you are starting to feel worse, it's important to have a place to remind you of what you did to get better. When you are starting to feel out of sorts, you can often trace it back to not doing something on your Daily Maintenance List.

A Daily Maintenance List may seem silly or simplistic and you may be tempted to skip or skim over it. However, most people find that it is the most important part of their whole plan.

On the first tab write Daily Maintenance List. Insert it in the binder followed by several sheets of filler paper.

On the first page, describe yourself when you are feeling all right. Do it in list form. Some descriptive words that others have used are:

bright	happy
cheerful	enjoy crowds
talkative	dramatic
outgoing	flamboyant
boisterous	athletic
a chatterbox	optimistic
active	reasonable
energetic	responsible
humorous	industrious
a jokester	curious

supportive	introverted
easy to get along with	withdrawn
argumentative	reserved
difficult	retiring
compulsive	supple
impulsive	breathe easily
content	a fast learner
peaceful	contemplative
calm	competent
quiet	capable

When you are not feeling well, it helps to have a reminder of what "being well" feels like.

Use the next page to make a list of things you know you need to do for yourself every day to keep yourself feeling alright. They are different for each of us.

Following are some ideas (change the amounts and times to meet your own needs):

- eat three healthy meals and three healthy snacks
- drink at least six-8 ounce glasses of water
- avoid caffeine, sugar, junk foods, alcohol
- exercise for at least 1/2 hour
- get exposure to outdoor light for at least 1/2 hour
- take medications
- take vitamin supplements
- have 20 minutes of relaxation or meditation time
- write in my journal for at least 15 minutes
- spend at least 1/2 hour enjoying a fun, affirming and/or creative activity
- get support from someone who I can be real with
- check in with my partner for at least 10 minutes
- check in with myself: how am I doing physically, emotionally, spiritually

- go to work if it's a work day (some people write a separate daily maintenance list for days they don't, or do, work)

On the next page, (or several pages later if you used more than one sheet), make a reminder list for things you might need to do. Reading through this list daily helps keep us on track.

Do I need to (or would it be good to):

- get a massage
- spend some time with my counselor, case manager, etc.
- set up an appointment with one of my health care professionals
- spend time with a good friend
- spend extra time with my partner
- be in touch with my family
- spend time with children or pets
- do peer counseling
- get more sleep
- do some housework
- buy groceries
- do the laundry
- have some personal time
- plan something fun for the weekend
- plan something fun for the evening
- write some letters
- remember someone's birthday or anniversary
- take a hot bubble bath
- go out for a long walk or do some other extended outdoor activity (gardening, fishing, etc.)
- plan a vacation
- call my sponsor
- go to a twelve step meeting or support group

That's the first section of the book. When it stops working for you, you can tear out the pages and write a new list.

You will be surprised at how much better you will feel after just taking these positive steps on your own behalf.

CHAPTER 3

Triggers

Triggers are external events or circumstances that, if they happen, may produce symptoms that are, or may be, very uncomfortable. These symptoms may make you feel like you are getting ill. These are normal reactions to events in our lives, but if we don't respond to them and deal with them in some way, they may actually cause a worsening in our symptoms. The awareness of this susceptibility and development of plans to deal with triggering events when they come up will increase our ability to cope, and to avoid the development of an acute onset of more severe symptoms. It is not important to project catastrophic things that might happen, such as war, natural disaster, or a huge personal loss. If those things were to occur, you would use the actions you describe in the triggers action plan more often and increase the length of time you use them. When listing your triggers, write those that are more possible or sure to occur, or which may already be occurring in your life.

On the next tab write "Triggers" and put in several sheets of binder paper.

On the first page, write down those things that, if they happened, might cause an increase in your symptoms. They may have triggered or increased symptoms in the past.

"If any of the following events or circumstances come up, I will do some of the activities listed on the next page to help keep my symptoms from increasing:"

> anniversary dates of losses or trauma
> traumatic news events
> being very over-tired

work stress
family friction
relationship ending
spending too much time alone
being judged or criticized
being teased or put-down
financial problems
physical illness
sexual harassment
hateful outbursts by others
aggressive-sounding noises (sustained)
being the scapegoat
being condemned/ shunned by other(s)
being around an abuser, or someone who reminds
   me of a past abuser
things that remind me of abandonment or
   deprivation
intimacy
excessive stress
someone trying to tell me how to run my life
self blame
extreme guilt (from saying "No", etc.)
substance abuse

On the next page, develop a plan of what you can do if your triggers come up to keep them from becoming more serious symptoms. Include things that have worked for you in the past and ideas you have learned from others as well as ideas from the appendix.

Sample Plan

If any of my triggers come up, I will do the following:

- make sure I do everything on my daily mainte-nance program
- call a support person and ask them to listen while I talk through the situation
- do some deep breathing exercises
- remember that it's okay to take care of myself
- work on changing negative thoughts to positive

- get validation from someone I feel close to
- some form of spiritual communication—prayer or meditation

In addition, some of the following activities might help:

- journaling
- going for a walk
- focusing exercises
- peer counseling
- seeing or talking to my counselor, case manager or sponsor
- time-out in a comfortable place
- enjoying a structured play time
- playing my musical instrument
- singing or dancing
- going to community activity
- vigorous exercise

CHAPTER 4
Early Warning Signs

Early warning signs are internal and may be unrelated to reactions to stressful situations. In spite of our best efforts at reducing symptoms, we may begin to experience early warning signs, subtle signs of change that indicate we may need to take some further action.

Reviewing early warning signs regularly helps us to become more aware of them, allowing us to take action before they worsen.

On the next tab write "Early Warning Signs." Follow that tab with several sheets of lined paper. On the first page make a list of early warning signs you have noticed.

Some early warning signs that others have reported include:

anxiety
nervousness
forgetfulness
inability to experience pleasure
lack of motivation
feeling slowed down or speeded up
avoiding doing things on daily maintenance list
being uncaring
avoiding others or isolating
being obsessed with something that doesn't really
   matter
beginning irrational thought patterns
feeling unconnected to my body
increased irritability
increased negativity
increase in smoking
not keeping appointments

spending money on unneeded items
impulsivity
poor motor coordination with no physical reason
aches and pains
dizziness
muscle cramping
excessive sweating
feelings of discouragement, hopelessness
substance abuse
passing exits on the interstate
failing to buckle your seat belt
not answering the phone
turning off the phone machine
overeating
under eating
weepiness
compulsive behaviors
feeling worthless, inadequate
secretiveness
controlling and/or manipulative behaviors
   (name them)
being too quiet
easily frustrated
feelings of abandonment or rejection
craving illicit drugs or alcohol
feeling compelled to take too much pain
   medication

Ask friends/family/neighbors for early warning signs that they've noticed.

The next pages are for your responses to early warning signs. If you notice these symptoms, take action while you still can. Using the ideas in the appendix and other techniques you have discovered on your own, develop a plan you can follow that will help reduce your early warning signs.

Following is a sample plan:

Things I must do

- do the things on my daily maintenance plan whether I feel like it or not
- tell a supporter/counselor how I am feeling and ask for their advice. Ask them to help me figure out how to take the action they suggest.
- peer counsel at least once a day
- do at least one focusing exercise a day
- do at least three 10 minute relaxation exercises each day
- write in my journal for at least 15 minutes each day
- spend at least 1 hour involved in an activity I enjoy each day
- ask others to take over my household responsibilities for a day
- go to (number) twelve step meetings

Things I could do if they feel right to me

- check in with my physician or other health care professional
- surround myself with loving, affirming people
- spend some time with my pet(s)
- read a good book
- dance, sing, listen to good music, play a musical instrument
- exercise
- go fishing
- go fly a kite

CHAPTER 5
When Things Are Breaking Down

In spite of our best efforts, our symptoms may progress to the point where they are very uncomfortable, serious and even dangerous, but we are still able to take some action on our own behalf. This is a very important time. It is necessary to take immediate action to prevent a crisis.

On the next tab write, "When Things are Breaking Down." Then make a list of the symptoms which, for you, mean that things have worsened and are close to the crisis stage.

Others have noted that the following symptoms indicate to them that "things are breaking down." Remember that symptoms vary from person to person. What may mean "things are breaking down" to one person may mean a "crisis" to another.

> feeling very oversensitive and fragile
> irrational responses to events and the actions of
>   others
> feeling very needy
> unable to sleep for . . . (you can specify
>   for how long)
> increased pain
> headaches
> sleeping all the time
> avoiding eating
> wanting to be totally alone
> racing thoughts
> risk taking behaviors, eg. driving fast
> thoughts of self-harm
> substance abuse
> obsessed with negative thoughts
> inability to slow down

bizarre behaviors
dissociation (blacking out, spacing out, losing
                time)
seeing things that aren't there
taking out anger on others
chain smoking
spending excessive amounts of money
  (say how much that means for you)
food abuse
NOT feeling
suicidal thoughts
paranoia

On the next page write a plan that you think will help
reduce your symptoms when they have progressed to this
point. The plan now needs to be very directive with fewer
choices and very clear instructions.

Sample Plan

If these symptoms come up I need to do all of the following:

- call my doctor or other health care professional,
  ask for and follow their instructions
- call and talk as long as I need to my supporters
- arrange for someone to stay with me around the
  clock until my symptoms subside
- take action so I cannot hurt myself if my
  symptoms get worse, such as give my medications, check book, credit cards and car keys to a
  previously designated friend for safe keeping
- make sure I am doing everything on my daily
  check list
- arrange and take at least three days off from
  any responsibilities
- have at least two peer counseling sessions daily
- do three deep breathing relaxation exercises
- do two focusing exercises
- write in my journal for at least one half hour

Other choices for the day might include:

- creative activities
- exercise

Ask myself, do I need:

- a physical examination
- to have medications checked

CHAPTER 6
Crisis Planning

Noticing and responding to symptoms early reduces the chances that you will find yourself in crisis. But it is important to confront the possibility of crisis, because in spite of your best planning and assertive action in your own behalf, you could find yourself in a situation where others will need to take over responsibility for your care. This is a difficult situation, one that no one likes to face. In a crisis you may feel like you are totally out of control.

Writing a clear crisis plan when you are well, to instruct others about how to care for you when you are not well, keeps you taking responsibility for your own care. It will keep your family members and friends from wasting time trying to figure out what to do for you that will be helpful. It relieves the guilt felt by family members and other care givers who may have wondered whether they were taking the right action. It also insures that your needs will be met and that you will get better as quickly as possible.

A crisis plan needs to be developed when you are feeling well. However, you cannot do it quickly. Decisions like this take time, thought and often collaboration with health care providers, family members and other supporters. Over the next few pages, I will share with you information and ideas that others have included on their crisis plan. It will help you in developing your own crisis plan.

The crisis plan differs from the other action plans in that it will be used by others. The other four sections of this planning process are implemented by you alone and need not be shared with anyone else; therefore you can write them using shorthand language that only you need to understand. But in writing a crisis plan, you need to make it clear, easy to understand, and legible. And while you may have developed other plans rather quickly, this plan is likely to take more time. Don't rush the process. Work at it for a while, then leave it for several days and keep coming back to it until you have developed a crisis plan that you feel has the best chance of working for you. Collaborate with health care providers and other supporters on developing this plan. Once you have completed your crisis plan, give copies of it to the people you name on this plan as your supporters.

Over the next few pages, I will share with you information and ideas that others have included on their crisis plan. It will help you in developing your crisis plan.

On the next tab write Crisis Plan. Insert several sheets of lined paper.

Part 1— What I'm like when I'm feeling well

The first step in this process is describing what you are like when you are well. Of course your family and friends know what you are like. But an emergency room doctor may think your ceaseless chatter is a sign of mania when you have been talking since the day you were born and will probably be talking from your grave. Or perhaps you are usually quite introverted. An unsuspecting doctor may see this as depression. Poor decision making or mistreatment could occur.

In the first section write words or phrases that describe what you are like when you are well.
Descriptive words might include:

talkative   laid back
quiet   retiring
outgoing   intellectual
withdrawn   humorous
adventurous   sensible
cautious   practical
outspoken   energetic
reserved   pale
ambitious

Part 2— *Symptoms*

You may find that this is the most difficult part of developing your crisis plan. Describe those symptoms that would indicate to others that they need to take over responsibility for your care and make decisions in your behalf. This is hard for everyone. No one likes to think that anyone will ever have to take over responsibility for them or their care. And yet, through careful, well developed descriptions, you stay in control even when things seem to be out of control.

Allow yourself plenty of time to complete this section. When you start to feel discouraged or daunted, set it aside for awhile. Ask your friends, family members and health care professionals for input. However, always remember that the final determination is up to you. It may take several months to complete this section.

Be very clear in describing the symptom. Don't try to summarize. Use as many words as it takes to describe the behavior.
Your symptoms might include:

> unable to recognize family members and friends
> incorrectly identifying family and friends
> severe pain
> inability to control body functions
> high fever
> unusual skin tone
> unconscious or semi-conscious
> uncontrollable pacing, unable to stay still
> very rapid breathing or seeming to be gasping for
>   breath
> severe agitated depression where unable to stop
>   repeating very negative statements like "I want
>   to die"
> inability to stop compulsive behaviors like
>   constantly counting everything
> catatonic—unmoving for long periods of time
> neglecting personal hygiene
> not cooking or doing any housework

extreme mood swings daily
destructive to property (throwing things, etc.)
not understanding what people are saying
thinking I am someone I am not
thinking I have the ability to do something I
    don't
self destructive behavior
abusive or violent behavior
criminal activities
substance abuse
threatening suicide or acting suicidal
not getting out of bed at all
refusing to eat or drink

On your crisis plan, list those symptoms that would indicate to others that they need to take responsibility for
you and make decisions for you.

Part 3 — Supporters

The next section of the crisis plan lists those people who
you want to take over for you when the symptoms you
list come up. They can be family members, friends or
health care professionals. When you first develop this
plan it may be mostly health care professionals. But as
you work on developing your support system, try and
change the list so you rely more heavily on family members and friends. Health care professionals are not consistently available. They move on to other positions.
Using natural supports is less expensive, less invasive
and more natural.

Have at least five people on your list of supporters. If you
have only one or two, they might not be available when
you really need them eg. on vacation, sick. If you don't
have that many supporters now, you may need to work
on developing new and closer relationships with people
by going to support groups, community activities and vol-
unteering. (See "Tips for Developing a Support System"
in the appendix.) But for now, list those supporters you
do have.

Following are some examples of attributes people want from those who take over and make decisions for them:

responsible
honest
sincere
knowledgeable
calm
compassionate
understanding
trustworthy

You may want to name some people for certain tasks like taking care of the children or paying the bills and others for tasks like staying with you and taking you to health care appointments.

When you list them, you may use the following format:

Name   Connection/role   Phone number

There may be health care professionals or family members that have made decisions that were not according to your wishes in the past. They could inadvertently get involved in your care again if you don't include the following:

I *do not* want the following people involved in any way in my care or treatment:

Name   Why you do not want them involved (optional)

Many people like to include a section that describes how they want possible disputes between supporters settled. For instance, you may want to say that a majority need to agree, or that a particular person or two people make the determination in that case. Or you may want some organization or agency to intervene on your behalf.

Part 4— Medication

List the name of your physician or physicians and your pharmacy along with their phone numbers and any allergies you may have.

List the medications you are currently using and why you are taking them.

List those medications you would prefer to take if medications or additional medications became necessary and why you would choose those.

List those medications that would be acceptable to you if medications became necessary and why you would choose those.

List those medications that should be avoided and give the reasons.

Part 5 — Treatments

There may be particular treatments that you would like in a crisis situation and some that you would want to avoid. For instance people have very strong feelings about electroshock therapy-both positive and negative. Let your supporters know whether or not you want this treatment. The reason may be as simple as "this treatment has or has not worked for in the past", or you may have some stronger reservations about this treatment.

You may have also found some alternative therapies that have helped as well as some that have not, eg. acupuncture, massage therapy, homeopathy. List those you prefer and those you want to avoid.

Part 6— Home/Community Care/Respite Center

Many people are setting up plans so that they can stay at home and still get the care they need if they are in a crisis by having around the clock care from supporters and regular visits with health care professionals. Many community care and respite centers are being set up around the country as an alternative to hospitalization where you can be supported by peers until your symptoms subside. Set up a plan so that you can stay at home or in the community and still get the care you need. You may need to talk with others about this and explore options that are available in your community.

Part 7— Treatment Facilities

Your supporters may not be able to provide you with the home, community or respite care. You may need a safe facility, you may be taking medication that needs to be monitored or you might prefer to take part in a program at a treatment facility.

Using your personal experience and information you have learned through your own research or through talking with others, list those treatment facilities where you would prefer to be hospitalized if that became necessary, and list those you wish to avoid.

Part 8 — Help From Others

What I need my supporters to do for me that would help reduce symptoms:

This section takes a lot of thought. You may want to ask your supporters and other health care professionals for ideas. What would really help when you are experiencing severe symptoms that would help reduce the symptoms?

Some ideas include:

> listen to me without giving me advice, judging me or criticizing me
> hold me
> let me pace
> encourage me to move, help me move
> lead me through a relaxation or stress reduction technique
> peer counsel with me

take me for a walk
provide me with materials so I can draw or paint
give me the space to express my feelings
don't talk to me (or do talk to me)
encourage me
reassure me
feed me good food
make sure I get exposure to outdoor light for at
    least 1/2 hour daily
play me comic videos
play me good music, (list the kind)
just let me rest
keep me from hurting myself, even if that means
    you have to restrain me or get help from others
keep me from being abusive to, or hurting others,
    do whatever you have to do to keep me from
    doing that

Include a list of things you need others to do for you, like
feed the pets, take care of the children and get the mail,
and who you want to do it.

Supporters may decide that some things would help that
would really be harmful. List those you have discovered
through past experience or those you feel could worsen
the situation. Some examples include:

forcing me to do anything
trying to entertain me
chattering
certain kinds of music
certain videos
getting angry with me
impatience
invalidation
not being heard

Part 9 — *When my supporters no longer need to use this plan*

When you feel better your supporters will no longer need

to follow this plan to keep you safe. Make a list of indicators that your supporters no longer need to follow this plan. Some examples include:

> when I have slept through the night three nights
> when I eat at least two good meals a day
> when I am always reasonable and rational
> when I am taking care of my personal hygiene
>   needs
> when I can carry on a good conversation
> when I keep my living space organized
> when I can be in a crowd without being anxious

You have now completed your crisis plan. Update it when you learn new information or change your mind about things. Give your supporters new copies of your crisis plan each time you revise it.

You can help assure that your crisis plan will be followed by signing it in the presence of two witnesses. It will further increase its potential for use if you appoint and name a durable attorney. Since the legality of these documents varies from state to state, you can not be absolutely sure the plan will be followed. However, it is your best assurance that your wishes will be honored.

You may want to use the following form to develop your crisis plan:

Crisis Plan

Part 1— What I'm like when I'm feeling well
Describe yourself when you are feeling well.

_____
_____
_____
_____
_____
_____
_____
_____

_____

_____

_____

_____

Part 2— *Symptoms*

Describe those symptoms that would indicate to others
that they need to take over full responsibility for your
care and make decisions in your behalf.

_____

_____

_____

_____

_____

_____

_____

_____

Part 3— *Supporters*

List those people you want to take over for you when the
symptoms you listed above are obvious. They can be family members, friends or health care professionals. Have at
least five people on your list of supporters. You may want
to name some people for certain tasks like taking care of
the children or paying the bills and others for tasks like
staying with you and taking you to health care appointments.

Name_____Connection/role_____
Phone number_____

Name_____Connection/role_____
Phone number_____

Name_____Connection/role_____
Phone number_____
Name_____Connection/role_____
Phone number_____

Name_____Connection/role_____
Phone number_____

Name_____Connection/role_____
Phone number_____

There may be health care professionals or family members that have made decisions that were not according to
your wishes in the past. They could inadvertently get
involved if you don't include the following:

> I *do not* want the following people involved in any
> way in my care or treatment:

Name_____
Why you do not want them involved (optional)

_____

_____

Name_____
Why you do not want them involved (optional)

_____

_____

Name_____
Why you do not want them involved (optional)

_____

_____

Name_____
Why you do not want them involved (optional)

_____

_____

Name_____
Why you do not want them involved (optional)

_____

_____

Settling Disputes Between Supporters

You might like to include a section that describes how

you want possible disputes between supporters settled. For instance, you may want to say that a majority need to agree, or that a particular person or two people make the determination.

_____
_____
_____
_____

Part 4— Medication

Physician _____Phone Number _____
Physician #2 _____Phone Number _____
Pharmacy _____Phone Number_____

List the medications you are currently taking and why you are taking them. Include the name of the doctor and the pharmacy.

_____
_____
_____
_____

List those medications you would prefer to take if medications or additional medications became necessary, and why you would choose those.

_____
_____
_____
_____
_____

List those medications that would be acceptable to you if medications became necessary and why you would choose those.

_____
_____
_____
_____
_____

List those medications that must be avoided and give the reasons.

_____
_____
_____
_____
_____
_____

Part 5 — Treatments

List treatments that help reduce your symptoms and when they should be used.

_____
_____
_____
_____
_____
_____

List treatments you would want to avoid.

_____
_____
_____
_____
_____
_____

Part 6 — Home/ Community Care/ Respite Center

Set up a plan so that you can stay at home or in the community and still get the care you need.

_____
_____
_____
_____
_____
_____
_____
_____

Part 7— Treatment Facilities

List treatment facilities where you prefer to be treated or hospitalized if that becomes necessary.

_____

_____

_____

_____

List treatment facilities you want to avoid.

_____

_____

_____

_____

Part 8— Help From Others

List those things that others can do for you that would help reduce your symptoms or make you more comfortable.

_____

_____

_____

_____

_____

_____

_____

_____

_____

_____

List those things you need others to do for you and who you want to do what.

What I need done   Who I'd like to do it

_____   _____

_____   _____

_____   _____

_____   _____

_____   _____

_____   _____

List those things that others might do, or have done in the past, that would not help or might even worsen your symptoms.

_____

_____

_____

_____

_____

_____

_____

_____

_____

_____

Part 9— Inactivating the Plan

Describe symptoms, lack of symptoms or actions that indicate supporters no longer need to use this plan.

_____

_____

_____

_____

_____

Part 10— If I am in Danger

If my behavior endangers me or others I want my supporter to:

_____

_____

_____

_____

_____

_____

_____

_____

_____

You can help assure that your crisis plan will be followed

by signing it in the presence of two witnesses. It will further increase its potential for use if you appoint and name a durable power of attorney.

I developed this plan on (date) _____

with the help of _____

Any plan with a more recent date supersedes this one.

Signed _____ Date _____

Witness _____ Date _____

 Witness _____ Date _____

Attorney _____ Date _____

Durable Power of Attorney (If you have one)

_____ Phone number _____

CHAPTER 7
Post Crisis Plan

The Post Crisis Plan is different from other parts of your Wellness Recovery Action Plan in that it is constantly changing as you heal. It is hoped that two weeks after the crisis you will be feeling much better than you did after one week, and therefore your daily activities would be different. After you feel that you are no longer in the post crisis time, you could go back to using your Daily Maintenance Plan and other parts of your Wellness Recovery Action Plan.

The need for the addition of an optional new section, Post Crisis Plan, to the Wellness Recovery Action Plan, was brought to my attention by Richard Hart, a Mental Health Recovery Facilitator from West Virginia.

Back in the late 1980's, I was hospitalized repeatedly for deep depression and severe mood swings. Those hospitalizations were somewhat useful. They gave me and my family a much needed break from each other. I got some peer support. I was introduced to some wellness tools, although that is not what they were called at that time, things like stress reduction and relaxation techniques and journaling. I was stabilized on a medication regime.

However, any positive effects from these hospitalizations were quickly negated when I got home. Twice, I returned to the hospital within two days of my discharge. Why? When I got home all my family and friends considered that I must be well. I was dropped off at my apartment and spent the next few hours alone. One time a friend who had promised to be there decided I must be napping, and didn't bother to call or come. There was no food. The space was messy and disorganized. I immediately felt

overwhelmed and totally discouraged. In addition, there
was a message that my employer expected me back at
work full time in the next few days.

No matter how you work your way out of a crisis, in a
hospital, in respite, in the community or at home, you
may also find that your recovery takes a few steps back-
wards after a crisis unless the journey out of this very
hard place is given careful attention. I have come to
believe that, for most of us, it takes as long to recover
from a crisis as it would to recover from any other major
illness or surgery. We need assistance and support that
can be gradually reduced as we feel better and better. It
makes sense that advanced planning for dealing with
that critical time would enhance wellness and more rapid
recovery.

As with the other parts of the Wellness Recovery Action
Plan, it is up to you to decide whether or not you want to
develop a Post Crisis Plan. If you decide you want to
develop a Post Crisis Plan, it is up to you to decide when
you will do it. Like the rest of the plan, the best time to
develop some parts of your Post Crisis Plan is when you
are feeling quite well. However, there are some questions
that can only be answered after the crisis when you are
beginning to feel better—like who needs to be thanked
and financial issues you need to resolve.

If you are hospitalized and you don't have a Post Crisis
Plan, you may want to develop one with your care
providers or on your own before you are discharged—a
kind of complete discharge plan. While you are in the hospital you may want to ask your care providers to explain
any possible discharge conditions and how these conditions would affect your post crisis plan if they were
imposed on you.

You may decide to develop your plan when you are working with a group or with your counselor. You could do it
with a supportive family member or friend. Others could
give you suggestions or advice if you wish, but the final
word should be yours. Or you could do it by yourself. It is

also up to you to decide whether or not you want to show your Post Crisis Plan to others. It may be a good idea to share your plan with people who you want to assist and support you as you heal.

You may want to sit down one afternoon and spend three or four hours working on your plan until it is finished. Or you may want to take your time—work on it a bit today, and a little more another day.

In developing your Post Crisis Plan, you may find it helpful to refer to your Wellness tools and your lists of what you are like when you are well, your Daily Maintenance Plan and your list of things you might need to do. You also may want to refer back to your Crisis Plan as you make plans to resume activities and take back responsibilities.

The forms for developing a Post Crisis Plan are quite extensive. As with other sections of your Wellness Recovery Action Plan you can skip over sections that don't seem relevant to you or that you would rather address at some other time.

You may want to revise your plan after you have used it—especially if certain things weren't as helpful as you thought they would be or plans did not work as you expected.

Post Crisis Plan

I will know that I am "out of the crisis" and ready to use this post crisis plan when I:

_____

_____

_____

_____

_____

_____

_____

How I would like to feel when I have recovered from this crisis:
(You may want to refer to the first section of your Wellness Recovery Action Plan—What I am Like When I am Well. This may be different from what you feel like when you are well—your perspective may have changed in this crisis.)

_____
_____
_____
_____
_____
_____
_____

Post Recovery Supporters List

I would like the following people to support me if possible during this post crisis time:

Who: Phone number: What I need them to do:
_____   _____   _____
_____   _____   _____
_____   _____   _____
_____   _____   _____
_____   _____   _____

If you are being discharged from a treatment facility, do you have a place to go that is safe and comfortable?
                    ___ yes ___ no
If not, what do you need to do to insure that you have a safe comfortable place to go?

_____
_____
_____
_____
_____
_____
_____
_____
_____

If you have been hospitalized, your first few hours at home are very important. Will you feel safe and be safe at home?   ___yes ___no
If your answer is no, what will you do to insure that you will feel and be safe at home?

_____

_____

_____

_____

_____

I would like _____
or _____ to take me home.

I would like _____
or _____to stay with me.

When I get home I would like to _____
or _____.

If the following things were in place, it would ease my return:

_____

_____

_____

_____

_____

Things I must take care of as soon as I can:

_____

_____

_____

_____

_____

Things I can ask someone else to do for me:

_____

_____

_____

_____

_____

Things that can wait until I feel better:

_____
_____
_____
_____
_____

Things I need to do for myself every day while I am recovering from crisis:

_____
_____
_____
_____
_____
_____
_____
_____

Things I might need to do every day while I am recovering from this crisis:

_____
_____
_____
_____
_____

Things and people I need to avoid while I am recovering from this crisis:

_____
_____
_____
_____
_____

Signs that I may be beginning to feel worse:
(examples: anxiety, excessive worry, overeating, sleep disturbances)

_____
_____
_____
_____

Wellness tools I will use if I am starting to feel worse:
(star those that you must do, the others are choices)

_____

_____

_____

_____

_____

_____

Things I need to do to prevent further repercussions from
this crisis—and when I will do these things:

_____

_____

_____

_____

_____

People I need to thank:

Person: When I will thank them: How I will thank them:

_____   _____   _____

_____   _____   _____

_____   _____   _____

_____   _____   _____

_____   _____   _____

People I need to apologize to:

Person: When I will apologize: How I will apologize:

_____   _____   _____

_____   _____   _____

_____   _____   _____

_____   _____   _____

_____   _____   _____

People with whom I need to make amends:

Person: When I will make amends: How I will make amends:

_____   _____   _____

_____   _____   _____

_____   _____   _____

_____   _____   _____

_____   _____   _____

Medical, legal, or financial issues that need to be resolved:
Issue: How I plan to resolve this issue:

_____   _____

_____   _____

_____   _____

_____   _____

_____   _____

Things I need to do to prevent further loss:
(canceling credit cards, getting official leave from work if
it was abandoned, cutting ties with destructive friends,
etc.)

_____

_____

_____

_____

Signs that this post crisis phase is over and I can return
to using my Daily Maintenance Plan as my guide to
things to do for myself every day:

_____

_____

_____

_____

_____

Changes in the first 4 sections my Wellness Recovery
Action Plan that might help prevent such a crisis in the
future:

_____

_____

_____

_____

_____

Changes in my crisis plan that might ease my recovery:

_____

_____

_____

_____

_____

_____

Changes I want to make in my lifestyle or life goals:

_____

_____

_____

_____

What did I learn from this crisis?

_____

_____

_____

_____

Are there changes I want or need to make in my life as a result of what I have learned?

_____

_____

_____

_____

If so, when and how will I make these changes?

_____

_____

_____

_____

Timetable for Resuming Responsibilities

Develop plans for resuming responsibilities that others may have had to take over or that did not get done while you were having a hard time, things like child care, pet care, your job, cooking and household chores.

SAMPLE

Responsibility: *going back to work*

Who has been doing this while I was in crisis: *co-workers*

While I am resuming this responsibility, I need (who):
Jane and Eric to *help with record keeping*

Plan for resuming:

Steps:
- *in three days go back to work for 2 hours a day for five days*
- *for one week go back to work half time*
- *for one week work 3/4 time*
- *resume full work schedule*

Responsibility: _____

Who has been doing this while I was in crisis:_____

While I am resuming this responsibility, I need (who):
_____to_____

Plan for resuming:

_____
_____
_____
_____
_____

Responsibility: _____

Who has been doing this while I was in crisis:_____

While I am resuming this responsibility, I need (who):
_____to_____

Plan for resuming:

_____
_____
_____
_____

CHAPTER 8

How to Use the
WRAP® Program

In order to use this program successfully, you have to be willing to spend up to 15 or 20 minutes daily reviewing the pages, and be willing to take action if indicated. Most people report that morning, either before or after breakfast, is the best time to review the book. As you become familiar with your symptoms and plans, you will find that the review process takes less time and that you will know how to respond to certain symptoms without even referring to the book.

Begin with the first page in Section 1, Daily Maintenance Plan. Review the list of how you are if you are all right. If you are all right, do the things on your list of things you need to do every day to keep yourself well. Also refer to the page of things you may need to do to see if anything "rings a bell" with you. If it does, make a note to yourself to include it in your day.

If you are not feeling all right, review the other sections to see where the symptoms you are experiencing fit in. Then follow the action plan you have designed.

For instance, if you feel very anxious because you got a big bill in the mail or had an argument with your spouse, follow the plan in the triggers section. If you noticed some early warning signs (subtle signs that your symptoms might be worsening) like forgetting things or avoiding answering the phone, follow the plan you designed for the early warning signs section. If you notice symptoms that indicate things are breaking down, like you are starting to spend excessive amounts of money, chain smoking or have more intense pain, follow the plan you developed for "when things are breaking down."

If you are in a crisis situation, the book will help you discover that so you can let your supporters know they need you to take over. However, in certain crisis situations, you may not be aware or willing to admit that you are in crisis. This is why having a strong team of supporters is so important. They will observe the symptoms you have reported and take over responsibility for your care, whether or not you are willing to admit you are in a crisis at that time. Distributing your crisis plan to your supporters and discussing it with them is absolutely essential to your safety and well-being.

If you have just been through a crisis, refer to your post crisis plan to guide you as you heal from this difficult time. When you feel you are ready, you can return to using the other parts of your Wellness Recovery Action Plan as you did before the crisis.

APPENDICES

The appendices contain introductory information on each of the following topics:

For more information on designing action plans refer to:

Copeland, Mary Ellen. *Winning Against Relapse.* Peach Press, Brattleboro, VT, 2001.

Copeland, Mary Ellen. *The Depression Workbook: A Guide to Living with Depression and Manic Depression.* New Harbinger Publications: Oakland, CA 1992.

Copeland, Mary Ellen. *Living Without Depression and Manic Depression: A Guide to Maintaining Mood Stability.* New Harbinger Publications: Oakland, CA 1994.

APPENDIX A

Developing, Keeping and Using
a Strong Support System

One of the most effective responses to symptoms is often reaching out to a very good friend, telling them how you are feeling or sharing an activity with them.

Everyone needs and deserves at least several key friends or supporters who:

- respect your need for confidentiality
- you like, respect and trust and who like, respect and trust you
- listen to you
- may have interests similar to yours
- let you freely express your feelings and emo tions without judging or criticizing
- you can tell "anything" to
- give you good advice when you want it
- allow you the space to change, grow, make decisions and even mistakes
- accept your good and bad moods
- work with you to figure out what to do next in difficult situations
- assist you in taking action that will help you feel better

If you have friends or supporters who do these things for you, you are very fortunate. However, you may feel that there is no one you can turn to when you are feeling bad. You may feel that there is never anyone you can ask for help, no one who cares about you. It's not hopeless. You can take action to change the situation.

Making friends is a skill like other skills—it can be learned. You may have trouble making friends and developing supporters for a lot of different reasons. They include:

- You don't feel good about yourself, so you can't imagine that anyone would like you. If you don't feel good about yourself and it keeps you from having friends and supporters, get a good book on raising self esteem (check out your local library) and work on it until you feel better about yourself.
- You expect your friends to be perfect, and so you can't find anyone who meets your standards. If this is true for you, work on changing this negative thought to "No one is perfect but there are many wonderful people who would like to be my friend and supporter."
- You are shy and don't know how to reach out to others. Practice being comfortable with others by joining a school club, church group or community group.
- You are sensitive to any sign of rejection, and react to it by giving up on the other person. Avoid giving up on people until you are absolutely sure they can't be supportive. Talk to others about what you are feeling, and encourage them to share how they are feeling. Work together so you can both feel good in the relationship.
- You have not had the opportunity to develop the social skills necessary to make and keep friends and supporters. If you feel this may be the case, discuss it with someone you trust. Tell this person that you have a hard time getting and keeping friends and supporters and ask them if there is something you are doing that is turning others off. Be prepared for them to give you and honest answer. Once you know what the problem is, you can work on correcting it.

Avoid:
- blaming others

- becoming overly dependent

Develop new friends and supporters by:
- joining a community activity or special interest group
- listening closely to others when they are sharing with you, everyone likes a good listener
- share with others openly and honestly
- accept yourself as you are
- accept others as they are, don't try to change them

Making the Connection

When you feel you have developed a special rapport with another person that feels like real friendship, i.e., the person seems as interested and as eager to spend time with you as you are to spend time with them, make a plan to get together. The first time you meet could be a low key activity like eating lunch together or taking a walk.

Don't overwhelm the person with phone calls. Use your intuition and common sense to determine when to call and how often. Don't ever call late at night or early in the morning until you both have agreed to be available to each other in case of emergency.

As you feel more and more comfortable with the other person, you will find that you talk more and share more personal information. Make sure you have a mutual understanding that anything the two of you discuss that is personal is absolutely confidential, and never make fun of what the other person thinks or feels.

Once you have met someone you like and who seems to like being with you, make plans to spend time together. Each time you get together, end that time by making a plan for the next time you will be together. If something comes up you want to share in the meantime, you can arrange a get-together by phone or in person, but always have something planned.

Key points about supportive situations

- Let the supporter know what you want and need. For instance, you may say, "Today I need you to just listen to me."
- Spend as much time listening and paying attention to your friends and supporters as they spend paying attention and listening to you unless you are feeling very depressed. Then be sure you pay attention to them another time.
- Spend most of your time with supporters doing fun, interesting activities together.
- Take turns suggesting and initiating activities.
- Keep regular contact with your friends, even when things are going well.

Keys to Keeping a Strong Support System

Once you have built a strong support system, how are you going to keep it strong?

1. Do everything you can to keep yourself well and stable. Make your wellness your highest priority. Others don't have a lot of patience with people who don't take good care of themselves.
2. Work on changing any bad habits you have identified that keep people from wanting to be your friends or supporters.
3. Be mutually supportive. Be there for others when they need you, and ask them to be there for you when you need them.
4. Try peer or exchange counseling with your friends or supporters. See the next section, Peer Counseling.
5. Have a goal of having at least five good friends or supporters. Make a list of your support team members with phone numbers. When we most need to reach out it is hardest to remember who our friends and supporters are, or to find their phone number. Have copies of the list of your supporters by your phones, on your bedside table and in your pocket.

APPENDIX B
Peer Counseling

Peer counseling is a structured way of getting the attention and support you need when difficult symptoms come up or when you are trying to cope with the stress of daily living. It provides an opportunity to express yourself any way you choose, while supported by a trusted friend and ally.

While peer counseling does not replace working with a professional counselor, therapist or mental health worker, it is a wonderful technique that can help you express your feelings, understand your problems, discover some helpful action you can take, and even to feel better. When used consistently, it is a free, safe and effective self help tool that encourages expression of feelings and emotions.

Peer Counseling Sessions

In a peer counseling session, two people who like and trust each other agree to spend a previously agreed upon amount of time together, dividing the time equally, addressing and paying attention to each other's issues. For instance, if you have decided you will spend an hour together, the first half hour is focused on one person and the second half hour on the other person.

It is understood that the content of these sessions is strictly confidential. Judging, criticizing and giving of advice are not allowed.

Sessions should be held in a comfortable, quiet atmosphere where there will be no interruption or distraction, and where the session cannot be heard by others. Disconnect the phone, turn off the radio and television, and do whatever is necessary to eliminate distractions. While most of us prefer sessions where we meet in person, they can be held over the phone when necessary.

The content of the session is determined by the person who is receiving attention—the talker. The talker can use their time any way they choose. It may include eager talk, tears, crying, trembling, perspiration, indignant storming, laughter, reluctant talk, yawning, shaking, singing , wrestling, or punching a pillow. You may want to spend some time planning your life and goals. The only thing that is NOT OK is hurting the person who is listening or hurting yourself.

Often, as the talker, you may find it most useful to focus on one issue and keep coming back to it despite feelings of wanting to avoid it. At other times you may find yourself switching from subject to subject. At the beginning of a session you may want to focus on one particular issue, but as you proceed, you may find other issues coming up that take precedence. All of this is up to you.

The person who is listening and paying attention needs to do only that, be an attentive, supportive listener. If they wish, if it enhances the process and if it is acceptable to the person receiving attention, the person who is paying attention can ask questions (but the questions must be asked in order to help the person focus, not to satisfy the curiosity of the listener) or encourage expression of emotion. The person who is paying attention must never demand anything of the other person. Full control must remain at all times with the person who is receiving attention.

In peer counseling, the expression of emotion is never seen as a symptom of a serious illness. Many of us feel that supporters view expression of emotion as meaning that something is wrong with us rather than as a vital part of the wellness process. We have been treated inappropriately for expressing emotion. We may have learned not to express emotion because it is not safe, thus interfering with our wellness process.

The person who is receiving attention (the talker) can make requests of the other person that assist in the process such as:

"Tell me what you like about me."
"Pretend you are _____ (parent, friend, employer, etc.) so I can safely practice telling her/him how I feel or what I want."

Counteracting Self Criticism

You may notice that when you are peer counseling, you say the same negative things about yourself over and over again. This is not helpful, and could even worsen depression or other symptoms. When you realize you are doing this, or the listener points it out to you, change the negative statements to positive ones and repeat these statements over and over again in the peer counseling session. Before long you will know that these positive statements are true and you will eventually feel better, even though at first it may make you feel worse.

Focusing Attention on the Present

When your symptoms are making you feel uncomfortable and keeping you from doing the things you need to do and the things you enjoy doing, it is best to focus counseling sessions on getting things back in order in your life and to focus your attention away from past issues. Sometimes it helps to focus your peer counseling session on the present, putting your attention on pleasant things and your life as it is now.

Keep the counseling session contained so that time outside counseling can be used to do things that make you feel good and to manage your life.

The session can be kept contained by the following activities:

1. At the beginning of a session the listener can reinforce the good that is happening in a person's life by asking them to share several good things that have happened in the last week (or day, or month, etc.). This provides a starting point for the session.

2. At the end of the session the person who is listening brings the otherpersonback to focus on the present by asking them to share something they are looking forward to.

APPENDIX C
Focusing

Focusing is a simple, safe, free, non-invasive yet powerful self-help technique that can help reduce symptoms.

The focusing sequence uses a series of well-defined questions or steps to help you focus on the real issue, the one of most importance at a given time, not what you may be thinking should be the real issue. It connects you with the feelings generated by that issue. When connection with the feelings are made and explored, a positive change in feeling is achieved. The result is an understanding at a new level that translates into feeling better and, often, reduction of symptoms.

Following is an example of a focusing exercise:

1. Get ready for a focusing exercise by settling down in a comfortable space and asking yourself, "How does it feel inside my body right now?" Search around inside your body to notice any feelings of uneasiness or discomfort and focus your attention on these feelings for a few moments.

2. Ask yourself, "What's between me and feeling fine?" Don't answer; let the feeling that comes in your body do the answering. As each concern comes up, put it aside, like making a mental list. Ask yourself, "Except for these things, am I fine?"

3. Review the list. See which problem stands out, that seems to be begging for your attention. It may be different from the one you thought was most important.

Ask yourself if it's ok to focus on the problem. If the answer is yes, notice what you sense in your body when you recall the whole of that problem. (If the answer is no,choose another problem that stands out and let the other alone for the time being.)

Sense all the feeling of the problem. Really feel it in your body for several minutes.

4. Let a word, phrase, or image that matches the feeling of this problem come into your mind.

5. Go back and forth between the word, phrase or image and the feeling in your body. Do they really match? If they don't, find another word, phrase or image that does feel like a match. When they match, go back and forth several times between the word, phrase or image and the feeling in your body. If the feeling in your body changes, follow it with your attention—notice it. Be with the feeling for several moments.

6. If you want, ask yourself the following questions about the problem to help yourself get a change in the way you feel:
- How does the worst of this feel in my body?
- What needs to happen inside me for this whole thing to change?
- What would feel like a small step forward with all this?
- What would feel like a breath of fresh air in this whole thing?
- How would it feel inside if this were all ok?
- What needs to change inside me for this to feel better?

7. Be with the feelings that came up for a few moments. Then ask yourself, "Am I ready to stop or should I do another round of focusing?" If you are going to stop, relax for a few minutes and notice how your feelings have changed before resuming your regular activities.

This is a very simple, safe exercise. It tends to become more effective the more you do it. Someone else can read the instructions to you or you can tape them. Before long you will know them so this won't be a problem.

APPENDIX D

Relaxation and
Stress Reduction Exercises

Use of relaxation and stress reduction techniques are an excellent way to help yourself feel better. Learn how to relax when you are feeling well. Practice regularly. It may even help uncomfortable symptoms from recurring.

Learning how to relax in our fast paced society where everyone expects us to be always working hard is not easy. The best way to do it is to take a stress reduction and relaxation course or class. They are often offered free at hospitals or health care centers. Watch the newspaper for announcements. You can also learn on your own by doing the exercises in this section.

In order to be effective, you must practice relaxation daily at a regular time. You will figure out for yourself the times when your house is most quiet and you would be able to take a 15 minute (or longer) break without interruption. Ask others in your household to respect this time by being quiet and not disturbing you. If you miss a time now and again don't fret. Just do the best you can. Practice relaxing until it becomes second nature, and until you can use it anytime you begin to feel nervous, tense or irritable.

Locate a space or several spaces in your home that are cozy, comfortable and quiet where you can be away from the concerns of your life. It may be in your bedroom. Relaxing outdoors in a secluded place in the woods, a meadow, by the ocean or on a mountain top is also a good idea.

When you notice uncomfortable feelings or symptoms, spend more time using your relaxation techniques and do it more often during the day. At these times, it is helpful to use an audio or video tape with a guided relaxation exercise.

Try some of the following relaxation exercises. See which ones help you feel better. (If any of these exercises make you feel worse, stop doing the exercise and try a different one).

Breathing Awareness —Lie down on the floor with your legs flat or bent at the knees, your arms at your sides palms up and your eyes closed. Breathe through your nose if you can. Focus on your breathing. Place your hand on the place that seems to rise and fall the most as you breathe. If this place is on your chest, you need to practice breathing more deeply so that your abdomen rises and falls most noticeably. When you are nervous or anxious you tend to breathe short, shallow breaths in the upper chest. Now place both hands on your abdomen and notice how your abdomen rises and falls with each breath. Notice if your chest is moving in harmony with your abdomen. Continue to do this for several minutes. Get up slowly. This is something you can do during a break at work. If you can't lie down you can do it sitting in a chair.

Deep Breathing—This exercise can be practiced in a variety of positions. However, it is most effective if you can do it lying down with your knees bent and your spine straight. After lying down, scan your body for tension. Place one hand on your abdomen and one hand on your chest. Inhale slowly and deeply through your nose into your abdomen to push up your hand as much as feels comfortable. Your chest should only move a little in response to the movement in your abdomen. When you feel at ease with your breathing, inhale through your nose and exhale through your mouth, making a relaxing whooshing sound as you gently blow out. This will relax your mouth, tongue and jaw. Continue taking long, slow deep breaths which raise and lower your abdomen. As you become more and more relaxed, focus on the sound and feeling of your breathing. Continue this deep breathing for five or ten minutes at a time, once or twice a day. At the end of each session, scan your body for tension. As you become used to this exercise, you can practice it wherever you happen to be in a standing, sitting or lying position. Use it whenever you feel tense.

The Inner Exploration—Pick a part of your body on which to focus all your attention. Explore that part of your body in detail with your mind. What are the sensations in this part of your body? How does it move? What does it do? Is it tense? If it is tense, practice relaxing this part of your body. You may want to choose parts of your body that tend to be tense such as the neck, shoulders, jaw, forehead or lower back. Or you may choose internal areas that tend to be tense such as the stomach or chest. Another idea is to focus on body parts that you rarely think about such as your toes, your elbows or behind your knees.

Being Present in the Moment—Most of the stress in our lives comes from thinking about the past or worrying about the future. When all of your attention is focused in the present moment or on what you are doing right now, there is no room to feel anything else. When meditating, all of your attention is focused on the present moment. When other thoughts intrude just turn your awareness back to the present. It is not necessary to be alone in a special When other thoughts intrude just turn your awareness back to the present. It is not necessary to be alone in a special place to focus all your attention on the moment. Try doing it when you are feeling irritated waiting in a line, stopped at a street light, stuck in traffic, feeling overwhelmed or worried. Notice how this makes you feel.

Progressive Relaxation— The purpose of this technique is to get you to focus on body sensations and how relaxation feels by systematically tensing and then relaxing muscle groups of your body. Make a tape recording of this exercise so you can use it when you need to. Be sure you leave yourself time on the tape to tense and relax your muscles.

Find a quiet space where you will not be disturbed. You can do it either lying on your back or sitting in a chair, as long as you are comfortable.

Close your eyes. Now clench your right fist as tightly as you can. Be aware of the tension as you do so. Keep it clenched for a moment. Now relax. Feel the looseness in your right hand and compare it to the tension you felt previously. Tense your right fist again, then relax it and again, notice the difference.

Now clench your left fist as tightly as you can. Be aware of the tension as you do so. Keep it clenched for a moment. Now relax. Feel the looseness in your left hand and compare it to the tension you felt previously. Tense your left fist again, relax it and again, notice the difference.

Bend your elbows and tense your biceps as hard as you can. Notice the feeling of tightness. Relax and straighten out your arms. Let the relaxation flow through your arms and compare it to the tightness you felt previously. Tense and relax your biceps again.

Wrinkle your forehead as tightly as you can. Now relax it and let it smooth out. Feel your forehead and scalp becoming relaxed. Now frown and notice the tension spreading through your forehead again. Relax and allow your forehead to become smooth.

Close your eyes now and squint them very tightly. Feel the tension. Now relax your eyes. Tense and relax your eyes again. Now let them remain gently closed.

Now clench your jaw, bite hard and feel the tension through your jaw. Now relax your jaw. Your lips will be slightly parted. Notice the difference. Clench and relax again.

Press your tongue against the roof of your mouth. Now relax. Do this again.

Press and purse your lips together. Now relax them. Repeat this.

Feel the relaxation throughout your forehead, scalp, eyes, jaw, tongue, and lips.

Hold your head back as far as it can comfortably go and observe the tightness in the neck. Roll it to the right and notice how the tension moves and changes. Roll your head to the left and notice how the tension moves and changes. Now straighten your head and bring it forward, pressing your chin against your chest. Notice the tension in your throat and the back of your neck. Now relax and allow your shoulders to return to a comfortable position. Allow yourself to feel more and more relaxed. Now shrug your shoulders and hunch your head down between them. Relax your shoulders. Allow them to drop back and feel the relaxation moving through your neck, throat and shoulders; feel the lovely, very deep relaxation.

Give your whole body a chance to relax. Feel how comfortable and heavy it is.

Now breathe in and fill your lungs completely. Hold your breath and notice the tension. Now let your breath out and let your chest become loose. Continue relaxing, breathing gently in and out. Repeat this breathing several times and notice the tension draining out of your body.

Tighten your stomach and hold the tightness. Feel the tension. Now relax your stomach. Now place your hand on your stomach. Breathe deeply into your stomach, pushing your hand up. Hold for a moment and then relax. Now arch your back without straining, keeping the rest of your body as relaxed as possible. Notice the tension in your lower back. Now relax deeper and deeper.

Tighten your buttocks and thighs. Flex your thighs by pressing your heels down as hard as you can. Now relax and notice the difference. Do this again. Now curl your toes down, making your calves tense. Notice the tension. Now relax. Bend your toes toward your face, creating tension in your shins. Relax and notice the difference. Feel the heaviness throughout your lower body as the relaxation gets deeper and deeper. Relax your feet, ankles, calves, shins, knees, thighs and buttocks. Now let the relaxation spread to your stomach, lower back and chest. Let go more and more. Experience deeper and deeper relaxation in your shoulders, arms and hands, deeper and deeper. Notice the feeling of looseness and relaxation in your neck, jaws, and all your facial muscles. Now just relax and be aware of how your whole body feels before you return to your other activities.

Guided Imagery— Guided imagery uses your imagination to direct your focus in a way that is relaxing and healing. Try the following guided imagery meditation.

Get in a very comfortable sitting or lying position. Make sure you are warm enough but not too warm and that you will not be interrupted by the phone, doorbells or needs of others.

Stare at a spot above your head on the ceiling. Take a deep breath in to a count of 8, hold it for a count of 4, let it out for a count of 8. Do that 2 more times.

Now close your eyes but keep them in the same position they were in when you were staring at the spot on the ceiling.

Breathe in to a count of 8, hold for a count of 4, out for a count of 8.

Now focus on your toes. Let them completely relax. Now move the relaxation slowly up your legs, through your heels and calves to your knees. Now let the warm feeling of relaxation move up your thighs. Feel your whole lower body relaxing. Let the relaxation move very slowly through your buttocks, lower abdomen and lower back. Now feel it moving, very slowly, up your spine and through your abdomen. Now feel the warm relaxation flowing into your chest and upper back.

Let this relaxation flow from your shoulders, down your arms, through your elbows and wrists, out through your hands and fingers. Now let the relaxation go slowly through your throat, up your neck letting it all soften and relax. Let it now move up into your face. Feel the relaxation fill your jaw, cheek muscles, and around your eyes. Let it move up into your forehead. Now let your whole scalp relax and feel warm and comfortable. Your body is now completely relaxed with the warm feeling of relaxation filling every muscle and cell of your body.

Now picture yourself walking in the sand on the beach on a sunny day. As you stroll along you feel the warmth of the sun on your back. You lay down on the sand. The sand cradles you and feels warm and comfortable on your back. The sun warms your body. You hear the waves crashing against the shore in a steady rhythm. The sound of sea gulls calling overhead add to your feeling of blissful contentment.

As you lay here you realize that you are perfectly and completely relaxed. You feel safe and at peace with the world. You know you have the power to relax yourself completely at any time you need to. You know that by completely relaxing, you are giving your body the opportunity to stabilize itself, and that when you wake up you will feel calm, relaxed and able to get on with your tasks for the day.

Now, slowly wiggle your fingers and toes. Gradually open your eyes and resume your activities.

The Relaxation and Stress Reduction Workbook (Davis, M., Eschelman, E.R. and McKay, M. Oakland, CA: New Harbinger Publications, 1988) will give you more information about stress reduction and relaxation.

There are many audio tapes that will guide you through relaxation exercises. These can be purchased at health food stores, book stores and through many mail order sources.

You can make relaxation cassettes for yourself by taping one of the relaxation exercises in this book, one from some other resource book or by developing an exercise which feels right for you. You may find it easiest to relax using an audio tape when you are experiencing symptoms or uncomfortable feelings.

Creative, Fun, Affirming Activities

Creative activities are a simple, safe, fun and affirming way to help reduce uncomfortable feelings and symptoms.

What are some things that you really enjoy doing, the kind of thing you really get "lost" in, when you are doing it you can't think of anything else? The list of activities that might help you to feel better is extensive. A few ideas include woodworking, knitting, sewing, building models, embroidery, cooking, photography and metal work. Perhaps it's fishing, reading mystery novels, playing the piano, cooking, playing with a pet, or quilting. Make a list of these things for yourself. Hang it on the refrigerator so you can refer to it, or put it in the front of your W.R.A.P. book

Any kind of artistic expression you are comfortable with can help you to feel better. Maybe it's acrylics, water colors, oils, crayons, magic markers, colored pencils, charcoal, or stick writing in the dirt. Perhaps you'd like to work with clay or one of the new synthetic clays. Maybe you'd like to carve something out of wood or even chisel away at a piece of stone—whatever would feel good to you. Gather together the materials you need and go to it. It helps to have the materials on hand so when you feel like using them they are available.

Remember, you are doing this to help yourself feel better and let out feelings and emotions. It is not to benefit someone else. It is not a piece to be judged or graded.

The hardest thing about these activities is getting started. Make a commitment to try an activity several times. If you enjoy it, make it part of your daily or weekly schedule. If you don't enjoy that one try another. Keep working at it until you've discovered at least several creative activities you enjoy.

For optimum wellness, spend some time every day doing one or more of these activities. You may want to spend a whole day or several days involved in these kinds of activities from time to time.

APPENDIX F

Journaling

People have kept diaries and written accounts of activities, events, dreams, thoughts and feelings since the beginning of time. Recently we have become more aware of the power of this tool in dealing with various kinds of emotional distress. Many people do it regularly no matter how they feel.

All you need to do is get some paper, a pencil or pen, and start to write. Write anything you want, anything you feel. It doesn't have to make sense. It doesn't have to be real. It doesn't need to be interesting. It's all right to repeat yourself over and over. Whatever is written is for you only. It's yours.

You don't have to worry about punctuation, grammar, spelling, penmanship, neatness or staying on the lines. You can scribble all over the page if that makes you feel better. Don't fix your mistakes. Just keep writing. Draw or paste pictures or words in your journal if you want. Doodle. Anything goes.

Most people choose to keep their journal writings strictly confidential. The privacy of the journal should not be violated by anyone. You don't have to share your writings with anybody unless you want to. Put a note in the front of your journal that says, "This contains private information. Please do not read it without my permission. Thank you!" Some people find it helpful and feel comfortable sharing writings with family members, friends, or health care professionals. This is a personal choice.

It helps to set aside a time every day for journaling. It may be early in the morning or before going to sleep at night. Spend as little or as much time writing as you want. Some people like to set a timer. You can write in your journal anytime—daily, several times a day, weekly, before you go to bed, when you wake up, after supper, whenever you feel like it—the choice is yours. You don't have to commit to keeping a journal for the rest of your life—just when you feel like it.

You can write at any speed you want, fast or slow. You can write as much or as little as you want. You can write poems, paragraphs, verse, novels, novellas, fiction, reality, your autobiography, someone else's biography, wishes, fantasies, dreams, beliefs, loves, hates, etc., etc., etc. It can be similar each time or very different.

Have a safe, private place to store your journal, like in the bottom of your underwear drawer or on a high shelf. Other people in your household should respect your right to a private journal.

If you have had a hard time starting to journal, try responding to some of the following questions:

> If my life could be any way I want, what would it
>   be like?
> What do I LIKE about myself:
> What is making me feel good today?
> What made me feel sad today?
> What made me feel happy and excited today?
> What are the stresses in my life?
> What makes me happy?
> Who are my favorite people?
> Write a letter to someone you would like to tell off
>   but you know it wouldn't be wise, or to someone
>   who is not available.
> Write a letter to yourself, pretending you are your
>   own best friend.
> List the best things that have happened this day
>   (month, year, in your life).
> The best thing that ever happened to me was:
> The worst thing that ever happened to me was:
> I want to be alive because:

APPENDIX G

Music

Listening to music and making music help people feel better. Think about the kinds of music that make you feel better.

When you are noticing uncomfortable feelings or symptoms, spend some time during the day listening to these kinds of music. Have available tapes or compact discs or know the local stations that feature music you enjoy.

Making music is also a good way to release feelings and pent-up emotions. Take some time to play any kind of instrument you enjoy playing. Remember you don't have to play perfectly or even well to enjoy playing. You don't need anyone else to critique for you. Just play for the sake of playing, for the fun of it.

Drums are great for this purpose. Put on some of your favorite music and then just beat to the rhythm. Enjoy yourself. If you don't have a drum, find something that it is okay to beat a rhythm on and use that.

APPENDIX H

Diet

You may begin to notice that uncomfortable symptoms begin or increase after you have eaten certain foods. The most common "bad guys" are sugar, caffeine, heavily salted and fatty foods. Try and become more aware of what you eat. Notice how you feel one half hour or more after you have eaten that food. Make dietary adjustments accordingly. You may want to consult with a nutritionist to find a diet that works well for you.

To feel your best, try following these healthy diet guidelines every day:

- Eat at least five servings daily of vegetables (about half a cup each). A big salad every day will help insure that you are getting enough vegetables. Also include at least one or two servings of fruit.
- Eat at least six servings of grains. This is easier than meeting the vegetable requirement. One slice of whole grain (dark) bread equals a serving, as does a bowl of cereal, pasta or rice.
- Include some protein in your diet, like fish, poultry or other meats, eggs, cheese, beans or soy products.
- Also include some dairy products in your daily diet, like milk, yogurt and cheese. Limit or avoid the dairy products that contain lots of sugar, like ice cream and frozen yogurt. They are great for an occasional treat but if you eat them often, you may feel worse. Don't get into the habit of getting an ice cream cone every day on the way home from school or work.
- Replace artificial, refined and processed foods that are low in food value with healthy natural foods.

APPENDIX I

Exercise

Exercise helps reduce unpleasant symptoms. When you exercise, you will notice that:

- you feel better
- you sleep better
- your memory and ability to concentrate improve
- your uncomfortable symptoms decrease
- you feel less irritable and anxious
- your self-esteem increases.

It is often difficult to exercise when you are not feeling well. Remember, even a few minutes of moving will help. Do the best you can. If you can't do it at all right now, don't give yourself a hard time. Begin as soon as you begin to feel a bit better. Listening to music while you exercise may help you feel more energized.

Do whatever it is you enjoy —walking, swimming, skating, roller blading, skateboarding, surfing, skiing, dancing, even outdoor chores such as cutting wood, raking, gardening, and playing with your pet can help.

You can do the same kind of exercise every day or vary it according to the weather, what you feel like, and things you need to get done. You don't have to join an expensive health club (although it is a wonderful treat if you can afford it). It doesn't have to be strenuous. Even a walk helps.

If you haven't exercised recently or have health problems that may affect your ability to exercise, check with your physician before beginning an exercise program.

APPENDIX J
Light

Have you noticed that you feel worse in the fall and winter or when there are several cloudy days in a row? If you answered yes to these questions and check off several of the following symptoms, you may have Seasonal Affective Disorder, more commonly known as SAD:

In the fall and/or winter I
____ lack energy
____ want to sleep a lot
____ have difficulty getting out of bed in the morning
____ am impatient with myself and others
____ crave sweets and junk food
____ have difficulty being creative
____ have difficulty concentrating and focusing my attention
____ have difficulty getting motivated to do anything
____ can't get as much done as usual

More people who live in the northern climates (or in the southern hemisphere in the south) have SAD than those who live closer to the equator. If you live in the north, it is even more likely that SAD or lack of light through the eyes is causing part or all of your problem with depression. In the winter the days are much shorter. We get up and go to school or work in the dark, and come home after dark. Sometimes we don't get out in the daylight at all.

Scientists have found that exposure to sunlight through the eyes helps some people who are depressed to feel better. Being outdoors in the light, affects the activity of neurotransmitters in the brain.

If you think you may have SAD, tell your doctor. He or she may be able to give you information on how to treat this disorder. If s/he doesn't know very much about it, ask him/her to refer you to a doctor who does. A physician who knows about light therapy will help:

- diagnose whether you have SAD;
- make sure light therapy is appropriate and there are no other medical conditions which need treatment;
- work with you to develop treatment that fits your schedule and lifestyle;
- help you in monitoring how you are doing;
- provide additional ideas on how you can get more light; and,
- give you needed encouragement and support.

There are some simple, safe, effective things that you can do to help yourself feel better if you have SAD.

1. Spend at least a half hour outside each day even on cloudy days. If you are at school or work, try to spend some time outside during your lunch hour. Glasses, sunglasses or contact lenses will block some of the sunlight you need. If you can't see well enough to go for a walk or be involved in some other outdoor activity without them, sit on a bench eating your lunch or talking to a friend.

2. Gazing at the sky helps, but never look directly at sun. The amount of light you get outside is enhanced by reflection off of snow and reduced by reflection off dark objects such as buildings and trees.

3. Keep your indoor space well lit. Have plenty of lights on. Let in as much outdoor light as possible. Spend as much time as you can in spaces near windows.

4. Consider using a light box.

Some people notice almost immediate relief of symptoms when they begin increasing the amount of light they get through their eyes. It usually takes from 4 to 5 days to work, but may take up to 2 weeks. If you don't feel any better after 2 weeks of treatment with light therapy, your problem is probably not SAD.

Tanning booths which only shed light on the skin are not recommended for light therapy.

For more information on SAD, write or call:

National Organization for SAD
PO Box 451
Vienna, VA 22180

Society for Light Treatment and Biological Rhythms
PO Box 478
Wilsonville, OR 79070
(503) 694-2404

National Institute of Mental Health
Building 10, Room 4S-230
9000 Rockville Pike
Rockville, MD 20892
(301)496-2141

APPENDIX K

Getting a Good Nights Sleep

A good night's sleep will help you feel better. Six to eight hours of sleep a night is enough for most people. (If you sleep too much, you will feel worse).

The following tips will help you get a good night's sleep every night.

- Go to bed at the same time every night and get up at the same time every morning. If you get to bed later than usual, get up at the same time anyway. You can take a nap later in the day.
- Avoid "sleeping in." It will make you feel worse.
- Avoid or limit the amount of caffeine in your diet. Coffee and tea are not the only culprits. There is enough caffeine in chocolate, some soft drinks and some pain killers to interfere with sleep.
- Avoid the use of nicotine. It is a stimulant. If you cannot give up your smoking habit right now, avoid smoking two to three hours before bedtime.
- Avoid the use of alcohol. While it may help you fall asleep, it will disturb your sleep later and may cause you to awaken early.
- Eat on a regular schedule and avoid a heavy meal prior to going to bed. Don't skip any meals.
- Eat plenty of dairy foods. They contain calcium that helps you sleep. If you can't eat dairy foods, talk to your doctor about calcium supplementation.
- Exercise daily but avoid strenuous or invigrating activity before going to bed.
- When you are trying to get to sleep, play soothing music on a tape or disc that shuts off automatically .

- Focus your attention on your breathing and repeat the words "in" and "out" silently as you breathe.
- Read a non-stimulating book or watch a calm television program before going to bed.
- Write in your journal about anything and everything until you feel too tired to write anymore.
- A turkey sandwich and a glass of milk before bedtime raises your serotonin level (a neurotransmitter) and makes you drowsy.
- A warm bath or shower before going to bed may help you sleep.
- Your local health food store carries a variety of sleep enhancing herbs, and homeopathic preparations that may help you get a good nights sleep.
- A drop of lavender oil on your pillow is relaxing and helps induce sleep.
- If menopausal symptoms such as hot flashes and night sweats are interfering with your sleep, see your health care professional for hormonal or herbal aids.

Facilitator
Training Manual

Mental Health Recovery
Including
Wellness **R**ecovery **A**ction **P**lan®
Curriculum
By Mary Ellen Copeland, PhD

The *Facilitator Training Manual* is an invaluable resource for anyone who is committed to sharing mental health self-help recovery information.

This comprehensive curriculum package includes a DVD with three videos featuring Mary Ellen, and:

- **Section 1:** Instructions for teaching recovery and WRAP®. Includes Values and Ethics.
- **Section 2:** Slides for workshop presentations. Thumbnail sketches and CD.
- **Section 3:** Activities, Handouts, Discussion Topics
- **Section 4:** Mental Health Recovery and WRAP® Group Model
- **Section 5:** Enhancing Learning Opportunities in WRAP groups

The Manual offers detailed information about facilitating Mental Health Recovery and WRAP® groups. The best preparation for this work is to develop your own personal WRAP® and to attend Facilitator Training offered by The Copeland Center for Wellness and Recovery, or by a Copeland Center certified Advanced Facilitator. For more information on becoming a certified Mental Health Recovery Educator and Wellness Recovery Action Plan Facilitator, call The Copeland Center office at 1-802-254-5335, or email: info@copelandcenter.com.

Facilitator Manual: Mental Health Recovery including WRAP _____ copies at $129.00

Subtotal $ _____

Shipping/Handling: total # curriculum x $10.00 per item _____

Total amount due _____

Name _____

Address _____

City and State _____ Zip _____

Phone _____ e-mail _____

Make checks payable to Mary Ellen Copeland.

( ) Mastercard ( ) Visa Card # _____ Expires _____

Mail order to: Mary Ellen Copeland, PO Box 301, West Dummerston, VT 05357-0301

Phone 802-254-2092   FAX 802-257-7499

E-mail: books@mentalhealthrecovery.com Website: www.mentalhealthrecovery.com

Announcing: A New Mental Health Recovery Resource

WRAP and Peer Support Manual: Personal, Group and Program Development
Co-authored by Mary Ellen Copeland and Shery Mead

Increase the effectiveness of your peer support and WRAP initiatives with this new manual. Mary Ellen Copeland, author of the well known *Depression Workbook* and *Wellness Recovery Action Planning*, and Shery Mead, who is at the forefront of evolving peer support practice, have joined forces to create this powerful manual. This book has the potential for creating great change in the way we do things in our own lives and in the way we work with others.

Why WRAP and Peer Support together? Peer support is about doing our relationships with others in new and different ways that promote growth, recovery and wellness. WRAP is about doing our life in new and different ways that promote growth, recovery and wellness. By combining the two, the skills and strategies that we discover in peer support can become part of our WRAP and the skills and strategies we discover as we learn about and use WRAP can assist us in peer support. The combination of WRAP and peer support can be incredibly powerful in helping us grow, learn from each other, and challenge each other beyond what we thought we were capable of. Using peer support theory, we can begin to use WRAP to help each other discover the context within which we've learned about ourselves, and then help each other develop plans that build a new life "story."

Self-Help Resources by Mary Ellen Copeland

Books

The Depression Workbook: A Guide to Living with Depression and Manic Depression Second Edition ....$19.95 x _____

Fibromyalgia and Chronic Myofascial Pain Syndrome: A Survival Manual with Devin Starlanyl ....$19.95 x _____

Healing the Trauma of Abuse: A Women's Workbook with Maxine Harris, Ph.D. ....$24.95 x _____

Living Without Depression and Manic Depression: A Guide to Maintaining Mood Stability...............................$21.95 x _____

The Loneliness Workbook ....$16.95 x _____

Recovering from Depression: A Workbook for Teens with Stuart Copans, MD...$24.95 x _____

The Worry Control Workbook................................$16.95 x _____

WRAP: Wellness Recovery Action Plan ....$10.00 x _____

WRAP for People with Dual Diagnosis...............................$10.00 x _____

Plan de Acción para la Recuperación del Bienestar...........$10.00 x _____

Quantity pricing for the above WRAP books: 1-9 copies - $10 each
10-99 copies - $8 each • 100+ copies - $7 each

WRAP for Veterans and People in the Military...................$6.00 x _____

A WRAP Workbook for Kids ....$12.00 x _____

Shipping for all WRAP books: $4 for one WRAP book, plus $0.50 for each add'l copy

The WRAP Story ....$19.95 x _____
First person accounts of personal and system recovery and transformation

WRAP for Your Computer, CD with printable worksheets and instructions, contains both adult & teen versions ....$19.95 x _____

Winning Against Relapse: A Workbook of Action Plans for Recurring Health & Emotional Problems Expanded version of WRAP with suggestions for group work.....................................$16.95 x _____

WRAP and Peer Support: Personal, Group & Program Development with Shery Mead...$40.00 x _____

Quantity pricing for WRAP and Peer Support:
1-4 copies - $40 • 5-9 copies - $35 • 10-49 copies - $30 • 50+ copies - $25

Facilitator Training Manual: Mental Health Recovery including WRAP
Curriculum includes DVD w/three videos of Mary Ellen, CD of slides, WRAP book and complete
instructions for facilitating mental health recovery and WRAP groups............$129.00 x _____

Quantity pricing for Facilitator Manuals: 1-11 copies - $129 each • 12+ copies - $110 each
Manual shipping: $10 for first manual, plus $8 for each additional manual

Community Links: Pathways to Reconnection and Recovery
with Shery Mead - Program Implementation Manual & CD ... $70.00 x _____

DVD and Audio Resources

Creating Wellness Workshop, DVD ....$60.00 x _____
Produced by MIEP, contains all three workshop sessions:
Key Concepts for Mental Health, The Wellness Toolbox, and WRAP

Wellness Recovery Action Plan, DVD.................................$19.95 x _____

WRAP for Veterans and People in the Military, DVD.......$19.95 x _____

Wellness Tools, Audio CD..$19.95 x _____

WRAP: Step-by-Step, Audio CD..$19.95 x _____

Subtotal: $_____

Shipping/Handling:
$4.00 for first item, +$1.00 for each additional item: $_____
Please use special shipping rates listed above for multiple WRAP books
and Facilitator Manuals.

Total amount due: $_____

Name: _____

Organization: _____

Address: _____

City/State: _____ Zip: _____

Phone: _____ E-mail: _____

Make checks payable to: Mary Ellen Copeland

Credit Card #: _____

Expires: _____ 3-digit security code: _____

Mail order to: Mary Ellen Copeland
P.O. Box 301, West Dummerston, VT 05357-0301

Phone (802) 425-3660 ♦ FAX (802) 425-5580
books@mentalhealthrecovery.com ♦ www.mentalhealthrecovery.com

02/10

WRAP® and Mental Health Recovery Content Available Online

Maintain and Achieve Recovery Anytime, Anywhere

Mental health recovery and WRAP® e-learning courses are designed to increase your knowledge-base about mental health recovery. You can take these courses on the Internet at your own pace.

- Creating a Wellness Toolbox
- Developing a Daily Maintenance Plan
- Triggers and Triggers Action Plan
- Early Warning Signs and Action Plan
- When Things Are Breaking Down and Action Plan
- Advance Directive/Crisis Management Plan
- WRAP One on One

Develop Your WRAP® Online

So much of our daily activities take place on the Internet, so why not your WRAP®? Build Your Own WRAP® is a web-based program to develop, personalize and change your WRAP® online as your life changes. Special version is available for veterans and people in the military featuring video clips with Mary Ellen Copeland talking to veterans as they are developing their WRAP®

Key features include email reminders for users and ability to store and develop lists and plans in the following areas:

- Wellness Toolbox
- Daily Maintenance Plan
- Triggers
- Early Warning Signs
- When Things Are Breaking Down
- Crisis Plan
- Post Crisis Plan
- Using Your WRAP

Go to the Mental Health Recovery website www.mentalhealthrecovery.com to build your WRAP® and take WRAP® online courses today.

essential
LEARNING

www.EssentialLearning.com

800.729.9198

info@essentiallearning.com

Essential Learning is the largest provider of e-learning services to the human service industry and our e-learning partner that we worked with to create these online services. For more information about Essential Learning, go to www.essentiallearning.com.